The Clinician's Mirror

A Story of Projection, Self-Awareness, and Transformation for Clinicians

By

Mardoche Sidor, MD, Lorie Meiselman, LCSW-R, Karen Dubin, PhD, LCSW, the SWEET Institute

SWEET Institute Publishing
Transformational Books for a Transformational World

Published by:

SWEET Institute Publishing
New York, NY
WWW.SWEETInstitutePublishing.com

First Edition
Printed in the United States of America

ISBN (Paperback): 978-1-968105-04-4

Cover Design: SWEET Institute Publishing

Interior Design and Layout: SWEET Institute Publishing

For bulk orders, permissions, or media inquiries, please contact:
info@sweetinstitutepublishing.com

Unless otherwise noted, all stories and case examples in this book are either fictionalized or used with permission, and identifying details have been changed to protect the privacy of individuals.

SWEET Institute Publishing
Transformational Books for a Transformational World

Dedication

To the clinicians who dare to see—not just their patients or clients, but themselves.

To those who sit in the quiet ache of awareness, who welcome discomfort as a teacher, and who choose reflection over reaction.

And to the patients and clients—the courageous minds who unknowingly hold up the mirror—inviting us not only to witness their healing, but to walk our own path of becoming.

This book is for you, for your bravery, your humility, your humanity.

And for the precious, unseen work you do every day.

Thank you for walking with the mirror.

Thank you for walking with us.

Other Books by Mardoche Sidor, M.D; Karen Dubin, PhD, LCSW; with the SWEET Institute

- Journey to Empowerment
- Discovering Your Worth: Everything You Need to Feel Fulfilled
- The Power of Faith: A Harvard-Trained Psychiatrist Speaking on Faith
- The Psychotherapy Certificate Course: The Clinician and Coach Manual (Books 1–3)
- The Anxiety Course: The Workbook
- What's Missing
- NLP for Clinicians
- 50 SWEET Poems: Reflections on life, love and self
- The Power of Belief: How Ideas Shape Leaders, Nations and the Future
- The Courage to Care: Stories of Healing, Hope, and the Power of Social Work: Told by   Over 50 SWEET Institute Social Workers
- Transforming Team Relationships from the Inside Out: The SWEET Healing Circle for Agencies: Redefining Accountability, Collaboration, and Culture
- Remembering: The Journey Back to the Pre-Conditioned Self

Table of Contents

Preface
by Mardoche Sidor, MD

We enter this field with the desire to help—to alleviate suffering, to listen deeply, to hold space for the healing of others. And along the way, we come to discover a quiet truth: we are being transformed, too.

This book you now hold is not a clinical manual, though you will find deep wisdom for clinical practice within it. It is not a memoir, though it contains moments of raw vulnerability. It is not a textbook, though it is grounded in sound psychological and neuro-scientific truth.

What this book is—profoundly—is a mirror, and not just any mirror. It is the kind that doesn't distort but clarifies. It doesn't demand perfection—it invites awareness.

In these pages, you will walk alongside clinicians as they confront not just the lives of their patients, but the unexamined places within themselves. You'll witness the subtle, powerful dance of projection—the ways we all, unknowingly, cast our inner stories onto the world around us.

The beauty of this book lies in its honesty. It refuses to position the clinician as all-knowing. Instead, it honors the therapist as a human being in process—someone who listens not only with the ear, but with their authentic self; and in doing so, it reminds us that self-awareness is not a luxury in this work—it is the very foundation of healing.

Read slowly. Reflect often. Let this mirror show you not just how to help others—but how to see yourself, more truly, more gently, more fully. Because, as this book so eloquently teaches, the work of transformation begins within.

Mardoche Sidor, MD
Former Clinical Assistant Professor of Psychiatry
Quadruple Board-Certified Psychiatrist
Columbia Psychoanalytic Center for Training and Research
Medical Director, Urban Pathways

Reflections

by Lorie Meiselman, LCSW-R

The idea for this book was born from a simple but profound realization: what we react to in others reveals hidden truths about ourselves. As clinicians, we are trained to observe, analyze, and interpret the inner worlds of our patients and clients. But what about our own?

Every clinician has experienced it—that patient who frustrates us beyond reason, that client who evokes unexpected sadness, or the person who seems to awaken something familiar yet unsettling within us. These moments, often dismissed as countertransference, are actually doors to greater self-awareness, if we are willing to open them.

This book is not about rigid theoretical frameworks. It is a journey—one that follows multiple clinicians as they confront their own unconscious biases, unprocessed wounds, and emotional blind spots in their work with patients and clients. Through each chapter, we witness how projection operates in real time, how clinicians wrestle with their own pasts, and how the therapeutic process becomes a two-way mirror.

Each case, each reflection, and each revelation within these pages is an opportunity—to not only understand our patients and clients better but to understand ourselves in ways we may never have before.

For those who seek deeper insight into the subtle, often hidden forces that shape therapy, relationships, and the way we see the world, this book is for you. Because the work of healing is never one-sided. Because we do not only change our patients and clients; they change us too.

Lorie Meiselman, LCSW-R, LPC, AC

Reflections
by Karen Dubin, PhD, LCSW

In the ever-evolving world of mental health, we often focus on understanding our patients and clients—how they have been impacted by trauma, their behaviors, and their patterns. However, rarely do we really take a look at how our own reactions, emotions, and unconscious biases have just as much significance in the therapeutic process. This book is a necessary exploration into the world of projection—not only as a clinical concept but as a deeply personal and transformative experience for clinicians.

Through compelling narratives and authentic clinical experiences, it becomes evident that the act of helping others is intrinsically linked to the journey of understanding oneself. The clinicians in these stories do not simply diagnose, analyze, or intervene—they learn, grow, and change alongside their patients and clients. Their internal struggles mirror those of the people they serve, revealing the hidden dimensions of countertransference, self-awareness, and the shared human experience.

This book is more than a guide for clinicians—it is an invitation to see oneself more clearly, to embrace the discomfort of self-discovery, and to use that awareness as a tool for deeper, more meaningful therapeutic work.

For every clinician who has ever felt inexplicably frustrated, deeply moved, or personally challenged by a patient or client, this book provides the framework to turn those moments into insight, and those insights into transformation.

As you read, you may find that these stories do not only belong to the clinicians in them—but also to you. Because in the end, the world is a mirror, and what we see in others will always reflect back something about ourselves.

— Karen Dubin, PhD, LCSW

SWEET Institute & Private Practice

Introduction:

Therapy is often described as a sacred space, where individuals uncover wounds, explore emotions, and move toward healing. Yet, what happens when the very act of listening stirs something in the therapist? When a client's pain echoes a long-buried part of our own?

This book explores one of the most overlooked yet transformative aspects of therapy: the role of projection in the clinician's experience. As stated above, we will examine the ways in which our reactions to patients and clients—our frustrations, sympathies, anxieties, and attachments—are not random but highly revealing. They provide clues about our own unconscious dynamics, unresolved conflicts, and deeply embedded patterns.

Through the following chapters, we will:

- Meet clinicians who find themselves emotionally entangled with patients and clients in ways they never expected.
- Explore the psychological and neurobiological foundations of projection, countertransference, and the mirror effect.
- Learn how to turn self-awareness into a powerful clinical tool—not just for our patients and clients but for our own personal and professional growth.

As you read, you will be invited to reflect on your own experiences, to ask:

- Why does this particular patient trigger me?
- What do my emotional responses reveal about my past?
- How can I use this awareness to enhance the therapeutic process?

The goal of this book is not to "solve" projection or to eliminate countertransference. Rather, it is to embrace these moments as opportunities for deeper self-inquiry, growth, and transformation.

Because, in the end, therapy is not just about healing the patient. It is also about the ongoing evolution of the therapist. And the world will always reflect back to us what we are ready to see.

Concept and Structure

The book will follow multiple clinicians, each with their own unique clients, struggles, and internal conflicts. Through their work, they unknowingly embark on journeys of self-discovery, learning that their reactions to patients and clients reveal more about their own unconscious material than about the patients and clients themselves.

It's structured in three parts, unfolding like a journey—from first recognition to deeper embodiment to practical application.

Each chapter will be a standalone story, yet woven together with a larger, overarching theme: how projection operates in therapy, and how clinicians can harness it for personal and professional growth.

Setting the Tone

The book begins in a clinical supervision group. A mix of seasoned and early-career clinicians gather, each bringing a case that has been particularly triggering for them. The supervisor, a seasoned clinician with a depth-oriented, Jungian approach, poses a radical question:

"What if everything you find difficult about your patients and clients is really about you?"

The room falls silent. From here, the novel unfolds as we dive into the inner worlds of different clinicians and the patients and clients who act as mirrors for their unexamined selves.

Some Patient Dynamics

1. **Clinician (Perfectionist, Seeks Control)**
   - **Patient:** A chronically relapsing individual with substance use disorder who repeatedly "fails" treatment.
   - **Core Projection:** Frustration at "lack of progress" reveals her own deep-seated fear of failure and losing control.

2. **Clinician (Compassion Fatigue, Avoids Confrontation)**
   - **Client:** A highly aggressive, defiant adolescent who refuses to engage.
   - **Core Projection:** His fear of conflict stems from unresolved childhood trauma of living with an authoritarian father.
3. **Clinician (Deeply Theoretical, Struggles with Emotional Intimacy)**
   - **Patient:** A young woman with borderline traits who idealizes and then devalues her.
   - **Core Projection:** Vanessa's intellectualization shields her from her own fear of emotional vulnerability, mirroring the patient's own relational struggles.
4. **Clinician (Struggles with Moral Judgment)**
   - **Client**: A convicted serial offender with antisocial traits.
   - **Core Projection**: His intense disgust toward the client reveals a hidden part of himself that once longed for power and rebellion against authority.

Each story unfolds, showing how these clinicians initially blame their patients and clients for their emotional reactions but eventually turn inward, leading to breakthroughs that transform both therapist and patient.

Theoretical Foundations

While the book is story-driven, it subtly integrates foundational theories:

- **Freud & Countertransference**: Reactions to patients and clients as a doorway to unconscious material.
- **Jung & the Shadow**: What we most reject in others lives in us.
- **Cognitive Neuroscience**: The world is a projection of our internal state.

- **Mindfulness & Neuroplasticity**: Using projection as a tool for self-awareness and rewiring responses.

Writing Style & Narrative Tone

- **Lyrical yet clear**: Deeply psychological yet engaging.
- **Visceral storytelling**: Readers feel what the clinicians feel.
- **Humor & humanity**: To balance the depth, moments of humor and personal warmth will make the clinicians relatable.

Conclusion: The Ripple Effect

The book closes with each clinician reflecting on how their self-awareness has transformed their practice—not just in how they treat patients and clients but in how they see themselves.

One final supervision session ties it all together:

- The supervisor brings the group back to the original question.
- They now see that their most difficult patients and clients were their greatest teachers.
- The book leaves you, reader, with a profound question: *What if our greatest discomfort is the key to our deepest growth?*

Acknowledgments

This book is born from the countless encounters that have shaped us—those moments of discomfort, insight, vulnerability, and growth that take place not only in the therapy room, but within ourselves.

To the clinicians who show up—day after day—not only to witness the lives of others, but to examine their own reactions with honesty and humility: this book is for you. May you feel seen in these pages.

We offer deep gratitude to the many patients and clients whose courage has mirrored our own blind spots, challenged our certainty, and opened doorways to transformation. Though their stories here are fictionalized, the truths they reflect are real.

To our mentors and teachers—particularly those who taught us to pause, to feel, and to listen inward—we thank you for modeling the power of presence.

To our colleagues and fellow travelers in this work, who held space, offered insight, and kept us accountable to the very themes we write about here: thank you for walking beside us with compassion and integrity.

And to you, reader: thank you for your willingness to reflect, to explore, and to stay with the mirror, even when it cracks.

Part I: The World as a Mirror

Chapter 1: The Art of Seeing

Scene One: The Smile That Stung

"I just think you're doing great," she said, with the kind of bright-eyed optimism that could only be interpreted as patronizing.

Evelyn Carter nodded politely, but inside she recoiled.

The patient, Miriam, had just finished describing how her self-criticism was easing, how she had finally stood up to her boss without trembling. She smiled—genuinely proud of herself—and offered Evelyn the compliment.

"You've really helped me."

But Evelyn's chest tightened. A flash of discomfort. She pushed it down.

Why?

Later, in the quiet of her office, Evelyn sat with the unease. Something about that smile—warm, grateful—had stung.

And then it came.

It reminded her of her mother.

The same smile, the same words, always following periods of emotional withdrawal. Her mother had used compliments as band-aids. They didn't soothe; they confused.

Evelyn wasn't reacting to Miriam. She was reacting to a memory.

Miriam had unknowingly held up a mirror.

Scene Two: The Patient Who Wasn't the Problem

Amir Patel was known for his calm. He prided himself on staying regulated, even in the face of chaos.

But there was something about Jordan—a 23-year-old who never made eye contact, who offered only yes or no answers, who slumped in his chair as if therapy itself was a form of punishment—that made Amir want to scream.

"Maybe therapy isn't what you need right now," Amir had said, almost too quickly, at the end of their fourth session.

Jordan shrugged. "Maybe."

After Jordan left, Amir sat alone in the silence. What was that? Why the urgency to push him away?

He saw it clearly: Jordan's withdrawn energy felt all too familiar. It was the same helplessness Amir had felt with his younger brother, who had refused help until it was too late.

This wasn't about Jordan.

Jordan had stepped into a role in Amir's unconscious play—and Amir had reacted from a wound, not from the present.

The session had become a mirror.

Scene Three: The Praise That Felt Like Pressure

Lisa Moreno had just finished a session with a teenage patient who said, "You're the only person I can talk to."

It should have felt good. Instead, it filled her with dread.

Because beneath the praise was a familiar story: if I disappoint her, everything will fall apart.

Lisa had learned long ago—growing up as the emotional caretaker for a volatile parent—that being "the only one" came with strings. It was never just love. It was a trap.

And now here it was again.

Not in her life. In her therapy room.

The Unseen Dialogue

These were not isolated stories. These were the rule, not the exception.

Therapy is never just one voice speaking and another listening.

It is never just one past on the couch.

Two nervous systems meet. Two unconscious histories collide.

And always, beneath the surface, there is a silent dialogue of projection:

Who am I making you into?

Who are you unconsciously asking me to be?

What parts of myself am I seeing in you, and calling "yours"?

We don't just perceive our patients. We project onto them.

And they don't just show up with their own stories—they walk into ours.

This is the foundation of projection.

Not a flaw in the therapeutic process, but a feature of being human.

A mirror that reflects not only the other, but also ourselves.

The Foundation of Projection in Therapy and Life

From the earliest days of psychoanalysis, thinkers like Freud, Jung, and countless others pointed to an uncomfortable but liberating truth: we do not see the world as it is—we see it as we are.

The human mind is inherently interpretive. Every encounter, every interaction, every emotion we experience is filtered through the lens of our past, our unconscious patterns, and the emotional imprints we carry. Projection—the act of unknowingly attributing parts of our inner world onto others—is not just a clinical phenomenon. It is a universal human reality.

In therapy, projection takes on heightened significance. Every time a therapist sits across from a patient and client, both individuals bring into the room not only their present selves, but also their entire psychological histories. The therapist does not merely observe the patient; the therapist sees the patient through the composite lens of past experiences, fears, biases, unresolved wounds, and unconscious assumptions. Likewise, patients see their therapists through the lens of their own histories—sometimes idealizing, sometimes distrusting, sometimes recreating past relational patterns without even knowing it.

While the term projection may often be reserved for the patient's process, this book invites us to turn the mirror back onto ourselves. The projections that therapists experience—whether frustration, admiration, attraction, judgment, or even helplessness—are not random. They are invitations, guiding us directly to the places within ourselves that are yet unexplored.

What we call countertransference in classical psychoanalysis is simply the clinician's version of projection. Yet, too often, it is treated solely as something to manage, contain, or overcome for the sake of the patient's progress. What if, instead, we were to approach it as something more sacred—a message from the unconscious, pointing us toward our own growth?

In this way, every therapy session becomes a two-way street. Not because the clinician is making the patient responsible for their healing, but because healing, when done well, never flows in one direction. As we attend to our patients, we are also being asked to attend to ourselves.

In life, this dynamic is no less present. How often do we react emotionally to strangers, friends, partners, or colleagues without realizing that what we are truly reacting to is a reflection of something unresolved within us? The difficult boss who evokes shame may echo a long-forgotten parental dynamic. The admiration we feel for someone's confidence may reveal a part of ourselves we have disowned. The friend whose indecisiveness infuriates us may unknowingly touch the very uncertainty we avoid within ourselves.

Jung once said, "Everything that irritates us about others can lead us to an understanding of ourselves." In the therapy room, this is not a philosophical platitude—it is clinical gold. If we, as clinicians, fail to recognize this, we risk missing the deepest opportunities for change—not only for our patients but for ourselves.

This is the foundation of this book: to recognize that the world—and especially our patients and clients—will always, without fail, serve as a mirror. The work, then, is not to avoid the reflection, but to learn to see it with clarity and courage.

As you journey through the chapters ahead, you will meet clinicians just like you, navigating the delicate balance of helping others while discovering themselves. Through their stories, you will see how projection—when recognized and worked with consciously—can become a key not only to effective therapy but to authentic human connection and personal transformation.

Scene Four: When You Can't Stand the Patient

Elena Martinez was known for her compassion. Colleagues admired her ability to stay present even in the face of intense distress. But when Troy walked in—loud, overconfident, dismissive of therapy—something in her bristled.

"I'm only here because my girlfriend thinks I need to stop being such an asshole," he said with a smirk.

Elena smiled politely, but inwardly, she was seething.

His tone, his swagger, his mocking—he reminded her of the older cousin who had humiliated her throughout her teenage years. The same condescension. The same weaponized charm.

She found herself fantasizing about cutting the session short.

But Elena knew better. She had learned to pause when her reactions were strong. To ask herself not what's wrong with him, but what is this stirring in me?

She realized: it wasn't Troy that repulsed her. It was the part of herself that still hadn't forgiven the years of silence, the way she'd smiled through humiliation to survive.

Her urge to shut Troy down was really an urge to shut down an old wound.

And suddenly, everything changed.

Instead of correcting him, she grew curious.

Instead of defending against the projection, she stepped inside it.

And in doing so, she found her way back to the present.

Projection as a Compass, Not a Contamination

Every therapist is trained to monitor countertransference.

But rarely are we taught to trust it.

We are told to be aware of it, to bracket it, to manage it—always with caution.

As if our emotional responses are threats to the work rather than windows into deeper layers of truth.

But what if we stopped treating projection as a contamination of the clinical space, and began treating it as a compass?

What if every emotional reaction we experience—irritation, admiration, protectiveness, helplessness—were not just feelings, but invitations?

What if, instead of silencing those internal stirrings, we learned to sit with them, listen to them, and trace them back to their source?

When we do, something profound happens:

- We begin to see the patient more clearly—because we are no longer seeing them only through our projections.

- We begin to see ourselves more clearly—because we are no longer unconsciously hiding behind our clinical roles.

- And we begin to recognize the therapy room for what it truly is: a place where two psyches meet, dance, and reflect one another.

Every Reaction Is a Clue

You might be thinking: But what about boundaries? What about neutrality?

And the answer is: boundaries matter. Neutrality matters. But authenticity matters more.

Because our reactions are happening anyway. The question is not whether projection is in the room—it always is. The question is: *Are we using it blindly, or consciously?*

Every emotional response is a breadcrumb, a clue pointing us back to ourselves.

- That surge of anger?
- Maybe your patient is unconsciously playing out a role you've been cast in before—by a parent, a sibling, a partner.
- That sense of urgency to rescue them?
- Maybe it's not about their pain at all. Maybe it's about yours.
- That glowing admiration you can't quite explain?
- Maybe they're embodying something you've disowned in yourself.

If we follow the thread inward, we don't just gain insight. We gain freedom—freedom from reflexive patterns, freedom to be fully present, and freedom to show up as both clinician and human being.

The Clinician as Participant, Not Just Observer

Traditional models ask the therapist to observe. To hold the container. To be steady and clear. And yes, those are sacred responsibilities.

But we are never just observing.

We are always participating.

Our presence is not passive. It is active.

Our nervous systems are not on the sidelines—they are in the room, co-regulating, mirroring, absorbing, reacting.

The more we deny that, the more we project unconsciously.

The more we embrace it, the more we transform therapy into a space of mutual evolution.

In this model, the therapist is not just a technician.

You are a mirror. A witness. A participant in a living, breathing encounter.

This is the art of seeing—not just the patient, but the self.

Not just the story in front of you, but the one playing silently in your own background.

In the chapters ahead, you will meet clinicians caught in moments like these—where the emotional reaction is stronger than expected, where the impulse to blame, withdraw, or rescue is hard to resist.

But rather than turn away, they will turn toward it.

And in doing so, they will find something unexpected:

The projection is not the problem. It is the path.

Chapter 2: The World of Projection

Scene One: A Tale Older Than the Couch

It was during her first year of psychoanalytic training that Evelyn Carter first heard the phrase:

"The patient is always the patient, but the patient is also your mother, your father, your sibling, your younger self, and every shadow you have yet to meet."

The senior analyst had said it so casually, as if it were common sense. But Evelyn remembered scribbling it down, feeling both intrigued and unsettled.

At the time, it sounded like one of those poetic, mystical statements older psychoanalysts and therapists were known for. Yet, she couldn't deny that it stuck with her. Years later, as she sat with patient after patient, she began to realize — it wasn't poetry. It was simple fact.

Freud was the first to name it in formal terms. Projection. The unconscious act of attributing parts of the self onto others. He noticed how his patients spoke of him as if he were someone from their past — father, critic, judge, or savior — without realizing they were doing it.

Jung took it further. To him, projection was not just clinical. It was universal.

"We see the world not as it is, but as we are."

Jung dared to suggest that projection wasn't something only patients did — therapists did it too. In fact, he believed we all do it, all the time.

Not because we are broken, but because this is how the human mind works. The unconscious mind, vast and largely inaccessible, leaks out into the world. We see through it, whether we want to or not.

Scene Two: Two Worlds Collide

Amir Patel, midway through his third year of practice, was sitting with a patient who seemed to constantly provoke him. Carla was a 42-year-old executive who belittled every attempt at empathy. Every kind question Amir offered was met with cynicism.

"You don't actually care," Carla said one afternoon, arms crossed.

Amir almost flinched. How could she say that? He cared deeply. He had chosen this profession because he cared.

But then he paused.

Where had he heard that before?

It hit him.

His father.

Those same words had been thrown at him throughout child-hood whenever he tried to express concern. Amir's father, bitter and closed off, would reject Amir's help with the same tone, the same folded arms, the same chilling accusation.

Carla wasn't being difficult. She wasn't hostile. She was triggering a projection — not from her, but from Amir. His reaction was not to Carla's words alone; it was to the ghost of his father behind her.

And for the first time in weeks, Amir could breathe again.

The Science Beneath the Mirror

Freud and Jung gave us the language.

Modern neuroscience gives us the map.

Today, we know that the brain is a prediction machine. It does not passively receive information — it constructs it.

Cognitive neuroscience has shown that when we meet another person, we don't encounter them with a blank slate. The brain pulls from memory, emotion, past relationships, and implicit learning to make predictions about what we are seeing and what it means.

- The amygdala, the brain's emotional alarm system, scans for danger or familiarity before conscious awareness catches up.
- The prefrontal cortex organizes these signals into thoughts and interpretations.
- Mirror neurons, first discovered in the 1990s, activate not only when we act but when we see another acting. They create a kind of immediate resonance. We don't just see another person's gesture—we feel it as if it were ours.

This is the neuroscience of projection.

We are always, without exception, filling in the gaps with what we already carry inside.

Our reactions to patients — admiration, irritation, urgency, impatience — are not only about who they are, but about the internal templates we bring into the room.

Scene Three: The Patient as the Mirror

Lisa Moreno had never connected the dots until it was almost too obvious to ignore.

When Rosa, a young mother struggling with postpartum depression, missed her third appointment without notice, Lisa found herself composing an unusually cold voicemail.

Then she stopped.

Why was she so hurt?

Rosa wasn't the first patient to miss sessions. Why did this sting so personally?

In the quiet that followed, Lisa recognized it. It wasn't Rosa. It was her own mother's unpredictability — the canceled piano recitals, the forgotten birthdays, the deep disappointment Lisa had long buried under competence and professionalism.

Rosa had, unknowingly, stepped into the shape of Lisa's unresolved longing.

The mirror had been lifted.

And now Lisa could choose:

React from the old wound?

Or tend to the present moment with awareness?

We Are Always Seeing Ourselves

Jung wrote, "The psychological rule says that when an inner situation is not made conscious, it happens outside, as fate."

In other words, if we don't recognize our projections, we don't escape them — we simply live them, over and over, often unconsciously inflicting them on those around us.

For clinicians, this is not just theory. It is the invisible architecture of every therapy session.

We are always reacting — always interpreting.

The question is:

Do we see what we are actually reacting to?

Or do we continue to mistake the patient for the past?

When we learn to catch ourselves in the act, projection becomes more than just a risk. It becomes a path.

A path to greater authenticity, deeper presence, and ultimately, more effective therapy.

In the chapters that follow, you will meet clinicians who, like all of us, stumble, react, project, and — if they are willing — grow.

Because as you will see, the most powerful work we do is not just helping our patients navigate their inner worlds. It is learning to navigate our own.

Jung, Freud, and the Unconscious Mirror

Carl Jung once wrote, "Everything that irritates us about others can lead us to an understanding of ourselves" (Jung, 1959). For both Jung and Freud, projection was not merely a psychological trick—it was a portal to the unconscious. Freud (1911) identified projection as a primary defense mechanism, a way the ego disowned unacceptable desires or fears by attributing them to others. Jung (1953) took this further, describing projection as the outward displacement of the "shadow"—the repressed, forgotten, or rejected parts of the self. In this light, the world is not just a stage—it is a mirror. Our judgments, our emotional charges, even our attractions, are all invitations to remember. The unconscious seeks wholeness, and projection is its language. The goal is not to stop projecting, but to become skillful in recognizing what the projection reveals. Every moment of reactivity can become a moment of return.

The Neuroscience of Perception and Projection

Modern neuroscience confirms what psychoanalysts intuited over a century ago: we don't see the world as it is—we see it as we are. The brain constructs reality by filling in gaps, drawing on memory, belief, and emotional salience to shape perception (Bar, 2004; Pessoa & Adolphs, 2010). Perception is not passive reception—it is active prediction. The visual cortex, for example, is deeply intertwined with brain regions involved in emotion and memory, such as the amygdala and hippocampus. This means our emotional past directly colors what we perceive in the present. Projection, then, is not merely psychological—it is neurobiological. Our nervous system itself is organized to project inner states onto outer cues. We see threat where we once felt powerless. We see judgment where we carry shame. We see abandonment in the smallest silence. We are not just seeing— we are remembering, through the lens of the unresolved.

Why What We React to in Others Tells Us More About Ourselves

The things that trigger us in others often reflect unprocessed material within ourselves. Neuroscience shows that our emotional brain—the limbic system—responds far faster than the rational cortex (LeDoux, 1996). When we react strongly to someone else's behavior, tone, or presence, it is often because that stimulus has touched a preexisting neural pathway wired by past emotional experiences (Panksepp, 1998). From a psychological lens, this is what both Freud and later object relations theorists described as transference—the unconscious redirection of feelings from the past onto present figures (Freud, 1912/1958; Kernberg, 1975). In daily life, these moments are mirrors. What we cannot yet hold, love, or accept within, we will criticize, avoid, or judge outside. The brain's default is to externalize discomfort. But with awareness, each reactivity becomes a flashlight: illuminating the hidden, the unresolved, the remembered self asking to be seen.

Chapter 3: The Mirror Holds No Lies

Scene One: The Smile She Couldn't Trust

It was a Tuesday afternoon when Evelyn noticed it—again.

Miriam, her patient, sat across from her in their sunlit office, sharing a story about standing up to her supervisor.

"I actually said no this time," Miriam said, smiling. "It felt... weird. But good. I kept hearing your voice in my head, reminding me that I had a choice."

Evelyn offered the expected nod, the affirming "mm-hmm," but inwardly, something tightened. The praise didn't land. The compliment didn't feel gratifying. In fact, it felt irritating.

As the session moved on, Evelyn found herself subtly distancing—less present, slightly mechanical.

When the door finally clicked shut behind Miriam, Evelyn sat frozen. What just happened?

She replayed the moment: the smile, the compliment, the gratefulness in Miriam's eyes. Nothing was out of the ordinary. By all accounts, it was a successful session.

And yet, Evelyn felt as if someone had scratched an old wound.

As the silence of the empty office settled in, Evelyn realized—it wasn't Miriam's smile that bothered her. It was who that smile reminded her of.

Her mother.

Evelyn's mother had mastered the art of the ambiguous smile. The same gentle but distant expression, usually following periods of emotional withdrawal. When Evelyn was a child, that smile was the beginning of reconciliation—but also the end of explanation. It was a way of saying: Let's pretend nothing happened.

And now, sitting across from Miriam, Evelyn wasn't just seeing Miriam. She was staring at the ghost of her mother.

Scene Two: The Moment Evelyn Almost Missed

The next session with Miriam, Evelyn came prepared—not with interpretations, but with awareness.

As Miriam shared updates about her progress, Evelyn noticed the familiar smile emerge again. This time, instead of retreating, she stayed with it—noticing the reaction, feeling it without acting on it.

She realized something crucial: Miriam's smile wasn't evasive. It wasn't dismissing or pretending. It was genuine.

But Evelyn's reaction to it wasn't.

Her body was still expecting her mother's pattern: a forced reconciliation, a subtle invalidation. Evelyn was looking for something that wasn't there.

This was projection, alive and breathing in the session.

And Evelyn, now aware, simply breathed with it.

She didn't change the subject. She didn't push the feeling away. She stayed present.

And because of that, she noticed something else: Miriam softened.

For the first time, she leaned in and added, "I think I'm starting to trust people a little more. Including you."

Evelyn almost missed it.

Had she stayed caught in the projection, she might have overlooked this vital opening. But by staying present to herself, she became more available to Miriam.

This wasn't just therapeutic technique. It was human presence, unburdened by unseen ghosts.

Countertransference is Projection in Disguise

In supervision, Evelyn brought the experience to her mentor.

"You didn't have countertransference," the supervisor said, sipping her tea. "You had a mirror."

Evelyn tilted her head.

"You weren't reacting to Miriam. You were reacting to your mother, showing up through Miriam's smile."

Evelyn nodded, feeling the weight of recognition.

This is where many clinicians stop—they name it countertransference and try to 'manage' it.

But what Evelyn was learning is that projection isn't just something to manage.

It is something to learn from.

Miriam had given her more than clinical material. She had given Evelyn a chance to notice a pattern she had carried silently into every relationship, including her work.

Projection as a Teacher

Evelyn began to wonder: How many other patients had she subtly withdrawn from? How many smiles had she misread? How many gifts had she rejected out of unconscious loyalty to an old story?

This is the deeper invitation of projection—not just to understand the patient, but to understand ourselves.

Projection is the thread that, when followed, does not simply lead to clinical insight, but to personal transformation.

This is the first real gift Evelyn received through her patient—not something that came from technique or theory, but from watching herself react, from becoming curious about her own discomfort.

By attending to the mirror, Evelyn didn't just help Miriam move forward. She freed herself, too.

And the next session, when Miriam smiled again, Evelyn could finally meet it—not as a child reacting to her mother—but as a therapist present with her patient.

The Work Behind the Work

This is where the real work of therapy often happens—not in the intervention, not in the interpretation, but in the quiet, invisible labor of the clinician sitting with themselves while sitting with another.

The mirror holds no lies.

It reflects back not only the patient's story but the clinician's, too.

And if we dare to look, it shows us precisely where we are invited to grow.

Countertransference as a Tool for Self-Awareness

In clinical work—and in life—countertransference is often misunderstood as something to manage, suppress, or avoid. But in truth, it can be one of our greatest tools for self-awareness. Originally defined by Freud as the therapist's unconscious emotional reaction to the patient (Freud, 1910/1959), the concept has since evolved into a more nuanced understanding: countertransference reflects not only our personal history, but also what is being evoked intersubjectively in the therapeutic relationship (Heimann, 1950; Racker, 1968). When we feel helpless, irritated, overly protective, or emotionally stirred in ways that feel disproportionate, these moments are not clinical failures—they are invitations. What within us is resonating with the story in front of us? What pain, fear, or unmet need is surfacing through this interaction? Used skillfully, countertransference becomes a mirror—not just for understanding the person before us, but for remembering the parts of ourselves still waiting to be seen.

Chapter 4: The Echo in the Room

Scene One: The Patient Who Said Nothing

It was the fourth session.

Amir Patel sat across from Luis, a soft-spoken man in his early thirties, who had come to therapy for "general anxiety," though very little had been said since the intake.

Luis stared at the floor, tapping his foot in slow, rhythmic beats. Amir asked questions gently, waited in silence, made room. But still, Luis barely responded.

Today, when Amir asked how his week had been, Luis shrugged. "Fine."

And then silence.

Again.

Something stirred in Amir's chest. He nodded, maintained a neutral expression, but inside, a quiet rage was building.

Why even come to therapy if you won't talk? he thought. Why waste both of our time?

His jaw tightened, and he shifted in his seat. He said nothing, but the heat behind his eyes betrayed his calm posture.

This wasn't just professional frustration. This was personal.

But he didn't know why. Not yet.

Scene Two: The Ghost Behind the Patient

Later that evening, Amir sat at his kitchen table, replaying the session in his head. The resentment, the tightness, the urge to provoke Luis into doing something.

He opened his notebook and wrote a simple question:

What does Luis remind me of?

At first, nothing came. But then—like an old photograph rising from the depths—a memory surfaced.

His older brother, Sameer.

Sameer had spent most of their adolescence locked in his room, barely speaking. Withdrawn. Dissociated. He had been unresponsive to Amir's attempts to connect—first playful, then desperate.

Eventually, Amir had stopped trying. And that silence had calcified into distance, then anger.

Luis's silence wasn't unfamiliar. It was identical.

And Amir realized he wasn't frustrated with Luis.

He was still angry at his brother.

Scene Three: Making Room for the Echo

At their next session, Amir entered the room with a softness he hadn't brought before. Not because Luis had changed—but because Amir had.

He was no longer unconsciously trying to pull Luis out of silence. He was no longer taking Luis's withdrawal as a personal challenge.

He sat, quietly, and simply said, "It's okay if you don't feel like talking today."

Luis looked up, startled. His eyes met Amir's for the first time in weeks.

After a long pause, he said, "You're the first person who hasn't tried to fix me."

That moment changed everything.

It wasn't a breakthrough in the traditional sense. It was something quieter. Truer.

Amir had stopped reacting and started witnessing. And because of that, something in Luis had softened.

Not because the therapist pushed, but because the therapist stopped pushing.

From Control to Curiosity

So often, our impulse as clinicians is to do something.

When the silence stretches too long, we fill it.

When the patient withdraws, we coax.

When there's no progress, we try harder.

But what if these moments aren't therapeutic roadblocks?

What if they're reflections—of the parts of us that can't tolerate stillness, helplessness, or the echo of our own unmet needs?

Amir's frustration was not clinical data about Luis's resistance. It was an emotional flashback to a time when connection felt impossible and silence meant abandonment.

By recognizing this, Amir didn't abandon the room.

He reclaimed it.

He moved from control to curiosity.

And in that shift, something changed—not just for Luis, but for Amir.

The Unfinished Conversations We Carry

Therapists often enter the field with an unconscious mission:

To finish the conversations that were never allowed.

To be the helper we once needed.

To finally get someone to open up, stay, or care.

But when a patient reflects that same "resistance," that same silence, it doesn't just challenge our clinical skills—it stirs our own unsaid things.

And if we're not careful, we might confuse the past for the present.

We might try to fix what is not broken.

Or rescue what is not drowning.

The echo in the room isn't a mistake.

It is an invitation—to pause, listen, and recognize:

This isn't just about the patient. This is about me, too.

In the next chapter, we'll follow Lisa Moreno as she confronts her need to "win over" a patient who reminds her of the very doubts she carries about herself and the field.

Another mirror.

Another invitation.

Another step toward seeing what lies beneath the surface.

Chapter 5: The Mirror Effect

Scene One: Winning the Unwinnable

Lisa Moreno had always been admired for her warmth. She was the clinician people described as "easy to talk to," "comforting," even "effortless." It had never felt like effort — until now.

Sitting across from Jonah, a 37-year-old engineer referred after a depressive episode, Lisa could feel herself working overtime.

Jonah wasn't hostile — not exactly. He was detached. Every session, he'd show up and, without fail, make some sardonic comment about therapy itself.

"Do you ever actually help anyone?" he asked one afternoon, half-smiling.

Lisa forced a chuckle, but inside, she bristled. She tried to meet him where he was, to reframe, to empathize. Yet, every attempt seemed to roll off him. The more detached he was, the more desperately she tried to reach him.

And when he left that day, Lisa collapsed into her chair, exhausted.

Why do I care so much? she thought. Why do I need him to believe in this? Why do I need him to believe in me?

Scene Two: The Clinician's Secret Doubt

That night, Lisa lingered in her office, tracing the sharp edge of Jonah's words.

They were too familiar. Not because Jonah reminded her of a past patient—but because his cynicism echoed something within herself.

There it was: The secret doubt.

That quiet, hidden question she carried even after years of training, after dozens of successful cases:

Does therapy really work?

Do I really help?

Lisa hadn't asked herself these questions in years. But Jonah's skepticism wasn't just annoying — it was triggering.

He wasn't the problem.

He was holding up a mirror.

And in it, Lisa saw the part of herself that still feared she might be a fraud.

Scene Three: Letting Go of the Battle

The next session, Lisa decided to do something different.

When Jonah, as expected, smirked and said, "So, convince me again why I'm paying for this?" Lisa didn't jump to reassure him.

Instead, she leaned back and said, "You know, sometimes I wonder that myself."

Jonah blinked. His smirk faltered.

Lisa continued, "There are days when I wonder if therapy makes a difference. And there are other days when I see it happen right in front of me. But I don't think I can convince you. I'm not sure that's my job."

The room fell silent.

For the first time, Jonah wasn't deflecting. He looked almost... relieved.

"Good," he said quietly. "Because if you tried, I wouldn't believe you anyway."

Both of them softened.

Lisa had stopped trying to win. And in doing so, she had won something far more valuable — authenticity.

The Mirror Effect

Jonah's cynicism was not simply "resistance." It was a gift.

It forced Lisa to confront the part of herself that still questioned her own worth, her own faith in the process.

This is the mirror effect.

When we react to our patients, we are often reacting not to their words or actions, but to what they awaken in us.

And when we try to change the patient to resolve our discomfort, we lose sight of the real work.

But when we notice the discomfort, stay with it, and turn inward, we find the hidden gold.

The patient is not the problem.

The problem is the unresolved part of ourselves that the patient unknowingly illuminates.

And paradoxically, when we stop trying to fix, persuade, or control — we open space for the patient to change.

Scene Four: The Shift

In the sessions that followed, Lisa noticed that Jonah, without any deliberate push, began to engage more. His sarcasm softened. He spoke about his loneliness, his grief, and his deep distrust of others — including therapists.

But this time, Lisa wasn't desperate to win him over.

She was present.

And Jonah could feel it.

The pressure was gone.

Because Lisa had already won the battle that mattered most — the one within herself.

In the next chapter, we will return to Amir Patel as he confronts a deeper, more personal projection when a patient unexpectedly triggers unresolved grief.

This next story is where the dance of mirrors becomes undeniable.

Chapter 6: The Dance of Mirrors

Scene One: The Pull to Protect

Amir Patel wasn't usually thrown off by emotional stories. Over the years, he had sat with grief in all its forms: sudden deaths, chronic illness, the long, silent erosion of relationships.

But something about Maya was different.

Maya was a 26-year-old college student who came to therapy following a series of panic attacks and a recent breakup that had left her unmoored. From the start, she spoke with a quiet, almost childlike vulnerability. She apologized often. She clutched a tissue even before the tears came.

"I know I'm too much," she whispered. "I always am."

Amir felt it instantly — the tightening in his chest, the urge to reassure, to protect her from the shame she carried like a second skin.

He found himself speaking more gently, leaning forward, praising her for small things:

"You're not too much, Maya."

"You're incredibly brave for showing up here."

On the surface, it seemed like compassion. But beneath it, something else was happening.

Amir was protecting her from a pain he hadn't yet named — not hers, but his own.

Scene Two: Echoes of the Unspoken

That night, Amir couldn't sleep. Maya's words haunted him. I'm too much.

He thought about how he had responded — overcorrecting, softening, soothing. There was nothing wrong with empathy. But this wasn't just empathy.

This was rescue.

And when he let the silence stretch long enough, a memory surfaced.

His sister.

Tara had always been sensitive, emotional, overwhelmed by the world. And after their mother died, she had become even more fragile. Their father couldn't tolerate her tears, so Amir had stepped in.

He became her translator, her shield, her emotional anchor.

Until she left. Until the grief swallowed her.

Maya's pain was stirring a familiar rhythm — the dance Amir had learned long ago: protect, soothe, contain.

But therapy was not family. Maya was not his sister.

And this was not the past.

Scene Three: Breaking the Pattern

At their next session, Amir noticed the familiar urge rising again. Maya apologized for crying. He almost interrupted to reassure her. But he didn't.

Instead, he said, "When you say you're too much — where did you first hear that?"

Maya blinked, surprised. "I guess… from my mom. She'd say it when I cried. When I asked for too much attention. She'd just get tired of me."

Amir nodded slowly. "And when you say it now, is it your voice? Or hers?"

A long pause. Then: "Hers."

For the first time, Maya's tears came without apology.

And Amir, quietly, let them.

He didn't rescue her. He didn't reassure.

He simply stayed.

The Dance of Mirrors

This is what projection often looks like: not a grand psychological event, but a subtle, unconscious dance.

Maya brought her story — shame, fear of being a burden, unmet needs.

Amir brought his history — the protective role, the unfinished grief, the guilt he carried for not being able to save his sister.

And in that room, their histories began to mirror one another.

Not because either of them chose it.

Because this is what happens when two nervous systems, two stories, two sets of unfinished conversations meet.

The therapy room becomes a mirror — and in that mirror, we see not only the patient's reflection, but our own.

The Therapist as Mirror, the Mirror as Medicine

Amir didn't need to fix Maya.

He needed to recognize who he was becoming in her presence.

Once he did that, the space between them became something else entirely — no longer shaped by reflexive roles, but by presence, by clarity.

Maya could finally sit in her sadness without being rushed out of it.

And Amir could finally witness pain without needing to protect himself from it.

This is the dance of mirrors:

We meet a patient.

We feel something.

We react.

And if we're aware, we ask:

Who does this person become in my mind?

Who do I become in theirs?

And what old story are we reenacting together?

Once we begin to ask those questions, the work deepens.

Not just for the patient, but for the clinician, too.

In the next chapter, we'll meet Elena Martinez, whose carefully constructed calm begins to unravel when a patient challenges her definition of "resistance" — and forces her to confront the story she has long kept hidden.

Chapter 7: The Mirror Cracks

Scene One: The Patient Who Wouldn't Cooperate

Dr. Elena Martinez sat upright, hands folded in her lap, her voice even. Across from her sat Troy, 40 years old, court-mandated therapy, arms crossed and face unreadable.

Elena had worked with complex trauma survivors, psychotic disorders, and patients in the throes of grief. But nothing irritated her more than this:

Someone who didn't want to be there.

"Why are you here?" she asked gently.

"Because I have to be," Troy replied, leaning back. "And because everyone keeps saying I have a problem. Maybe if I sit here long enough, someone can check a box and we can all move on."

Elena smiled politely. Internally, her stomach tightened.

She told herself it was his resistance. His hostility. His refusal to engage.

But the truth was more complicated.

She wasn't just frustrated.

She was hurt.

Scene Two: The Uninvited Feeling

That night, Elena sat in her apartment, wine glass untouched, laptop open but ignored. She was still thinking about Troy.

It wasn't his words — it was the way he said them. Cold. Detached. Dismissive.

She had heard that tone before.

It took her a moment to place it.

It was her father.

The same dry indifference. The same emotional wall. The same signal that said, you're wasting your time.

As a child, Elena had spent years trying to connect with him — reading books he liked, pretending to enjoy his hobbies, waiting for the moment he'd soften.

He never did.

And now, sitting across from Troy, Elena wasn't just reacting to a patient.

She was sitting with a ghost.

Scene Three: The Crack in the Mask

At their next session, Troy was no different.

"I'm not going to cry," he said abruptly, as Elena gently invited him to talk about the recent loss of his brother. "That's not how I deal with things."

Elena heard herself respond before she could stop.

"You don't have to cry, but it's okay if you do."

Troy rolled his eyes. "You therapists and your feelings."

Her chest tightened again.

But this time, she paused. She noticed it.

She wasn't angry with Troy.

She was back in her childhood living room, listening to her father dismiss her vulnerability — again.

The mask cracked.

She exhaled slowly. "I'm not here to make you cry," she said. "And I won't pretend I know what you need. Maybe you're right — maybe I am reaching for something you're not ready for."

Troy blinked.

For the first time, he didn't interrupt.

He just nodded.

49

When the Mirror Breaks You Open

Projection doesn't always feel like projection.

Sometimes it feels like disappointment. Sometimes it feels like "resistance."

And sometimes — like in Elena's case — it feels personal.

Troy wasn't rejecting her.

But her body, her nervous system, didn't know that.

She had internalized rejection so deeply that even a detached sentence from a patient could reawaken the old ache.

And until she saw that, she was at risk of missing the moment.

Missing him.

The Therapist's Wound Is the Work

In training, Elena had been praised for her calm presence.

Her ability to stay composed in chaos.

But calm is not always clarity.

And composure can be a shield.

It took Troy's indifference to show Elena the wound beneath her professionalism — the one that had long gone unspoken, unexamined, unresolved.

The one that said: If I can just stay calm enough, I'll be accepted. I won't be pushed away.

Once she saw it, she didn't need to fight for Troy's engagement.

She could finally offer him something more honest:

A presence that wasn't pretending.

The Mirror Doesn't Lie, But It Can Heal

Troy didn't suddenly transform.

He didn't burst into tears or share his deepest secrets.

But something shifted.

He came back the next week. He leaned forward.

And when Elena made a joke — dry, subtle, like his own — he actually smiled.

Tiny moments.

But real ones.

Not because Elena had mastered a new technique.

But because she had stopped reliving her old story.

The mirror had cracked.

And through the crack, light came in.

In the next chapter, we'll begin Part II: Seeing Ourselves in the Other. The focus will turn from the initial recognition of projection to how this awareness ripples outward — shaping therapeutic outcomes, clinician growth, and the unfolding of true presence.

Part II: Seeing Ourselves in the Other

Chapter 8: The Ripple Effect

Scene One: What Changed?

Dr. Evelyn Carter couldn't help but notice something subtle — something she hadn't expected.

Since the moment she recognized how Miriam's smile mirrored her mother's, something had shifted. Miriam's symptoms had not vanished, nor had Evelyn suddenly discovered a therapeutic breakthrough.

But the room felt different.

The work felt different.

Miriam talked more. Her anxiety softened. Evelyn found herself listening — really listening — without subtly pulling away.

One afternoon, as Miriam described an argument with her boss, Evelyn caught herself feeling genuinely invested, no longer navigating the fog of her own projection.

And it wasn't just Miriam.

With other patients, too, Evelyn noticed herself hesitating less, leaning into moments of discomfort, holding silence without defensiveness.

What had changed?

She had.

Not by reading another manual.

Not by mastering another technique.

But by looking into the mirror.

Scene Two: Amir Notices the Shift

Dr. Amir Patel saw it too.

Since the realization with Maya — his patient who reminded him of his sister — Amir had felt lighter in sessions. His urgency to rescue was quieter. His listening deeper.

And Maya noticed.

"You don't seem so... I don't know, worried about me anymore," she said one day. "I don't feel like you're trying to fix me."

Amir felt a pang of humility. She was right.

By recognizing his own projection, Amir had changed the entire emotional atmosphere of the therapy.

And the ripple didn't end with Maya.

In subsequent sessions with other patients, Amir found himself curious rather than reactive. Where he used to fill silences, he now allowed them to breathe. Where he used to rush to comfort, he now let emotions unfold.

Patients felt it.

They relaxed.

They opened.

They trusted.

Scene Three: The Ripple Beyond the Room

For Lisa, the ripple wasn't limited to her office.

One evening at dinner with a close friend, she noticed the same impulse — the urge to convince, to win over, to be seen as valuable.

It wasn't just Jonah, her skeptical patient, who triggered this.

It was everywhere.

Her friend was describing a difficult breakup, speaking with resignation. Lisa felt the pull to prove that things could get better — to offer the perfect insight, the right advice.

But this time, she caught it.

She stayed quiet.

Present.

Trusting that her friend didn't need Lisa's brilliance — just her presence.

And in the silence, her friend sighed.

"I think I just needed someone to hear me."

The ripple was real.

Projection awareness doesn't just change therapy. It changes everything.

What We Bring Shapes What We See

The more the clinicians noticed, the more they realized:

- When they became impatient, it wasn't always about the patient's resistance.
- When they felt drained, it wasn't always about the patient's pathology.
- When they felt inspired, it wasn't always about the patient's progress.

It was often about what they were bringing into the room.

Their histories.

Their assumptions.

Their projections.

And when they changed — when they stopped reacting automatically — their patients changed, too.

Not because they made their patients change.

But because the space between them changed.

The Power of Naming It

Some of the most profound shifts didn't come from new interventions.

They came from clinicians saying, aloud or silently:

"I notice I'm feeling _____. I wonder what this tells me about me."

This simple act created space for the patient to be more than just a character in the clinician's unconscious story.

It invited the therapist to be more than just a reactor — to become an observer and a participant in a more conscious way.

And from that space, therapy became something more than problem-solving.

It became a shared act of truth-telling.

And the ripple spread — into every interaction, every supervision, every relationship beyond the therapy room.

In the next chapter, we will go deeper into how patterns, once seen, can begin to be broken — and how therapists learn to discern between the patient's story and their own.

Chapter 9: Breaking the Patterns

Scene One: The Familiar Pull

Dr. Lisa Moreno felt it again.

A new client. New case. Same sensation.

Melissa was in her late twenties. Bright, articulate, and—within minutes—apologizing for taking up space.

"I'm probably wasting your time," she said during their first session. "I know other people need this more than I do."

Lisa felt the tug — that reflexive need to reassure. To lean in. To make sure Melissa felt valued.

But this time, she didn't rush in.

She stayed still, curious.

What was this need to reassure?

Whose reassurance was she chasing? Hers—or mine?

Lisa realized something:

Melissa wasn't just a patient.

She was a pattern.

One that Lisa had lived before, played out unconsciously, and unknowingly perpetuated in the therapy room.

This time, she didn't reinforce the script.

She broke it.

"You know, I wonder where you learned to apologize before you've even said anything," she asked gently.

Melissa froze. Then slowly nodded.

"I guess... I've always done that."

And in that moment, something cracked open.

Scene Two: Amir's Realization

Dr. Amir Patel was reading over a case note when it hit him:

The dynamic he kept falling into with certain patients — especially those who reminded him of his brother — wasn't just emotional.

It was relationally patterned.

Patient withdraws.

He leans in.

Patient gets quieter.

He works harder.

Patient disengages.

He doubts himself.

He had been seeing it as resistance.

Now he saw it as choreography.

A dance learned long ago. A rhythm scripted by grief, loss, and helplessness.

And unless he became conscious of it, he'd keep dancing.

So at his next session with a patient named Reed — a quiet, avoidant man in his mid-thirties — Amir did something different.

He didn't try to pull Reed out of silence.

He sat in it.

Not as a test.

As a choice.

And after almost seven minutes of stillness, Reed spoke.

"I've never had someone wait like this before."

Scene Three: Elena's Undoing

Dr. Elena Martinez used to pride herself on being the "strong one."

Unshakeable. Grounded.

But lately, her patients were bringing something out in her — a low, humming anxiety just beneath her composed surface.

In supervision, she named it.

"It's like I keep attracting patients who shut down or push me away. And every time, I try harder to connect... which just seems to make it worse."

Her supervisor raised an eyebrow. "What would happen if you stopped trying?"

Elena froze.

Stopped trying?

She'd never considered that. Trying was her armor. Her identity.

That evening, she journaled:

What am I afraid will happen if I stop trying to be what they need?

And the answer came:

They'll leave. I'll fail. I won't matter.

There it was. The pattern.

Born from a childhood where love had to be earned, effort had to be endless, and being "enough" was always conditional.

Now, in the therapy room, she was unconsciously reenacting the same thing.

Until she saw it.

Named it.

Interrupted it.

The Power of Pattern Recognition

The patterns clinicians bring into the therapy room aren't flaws.

They are adaptations.

Strategies that once ensured survival — now silently shaping the work in ways we rarely notice.

And when patients unknowingly step into these patterns, they often play the role we most fear, most resent, or most long to redeem.

It isn't their doing.

It isn't our fault.

But it is our responsibility.

To notice.

To ask:

- What's familiar about this feeling?
- When else have I felt this way — outside of this room?
- What role am I unconsciously stepping into right now?

And then, most importantly:

To choose differently.

Working With, Not Against

Breaking the pattern doesn't mean eliminating emotion.

It means being aware of it — and working from that awareness rather than from the old reflex.

- When the patient withdraws, and we want to chase — we pause.
- When the patient attacks, and we want to defend — we stay open.
- When the patient idealizes, and we want to live up to it — we reflect, not perform.

This is the difference between reacting and responding.

Between being reenacted and being present.

And every time we choose awareness over reflex, a new pattern becomes possible.

For us.

And for them.

In the next chapter, we'll explore the space between clinician and patient — the invisible field where these dynamics play out.

Where silence holds story.

Where presence becomes intervention.

Where the true work of healing lives.

Chapter 10: The Space Between Us

Scene One: The Pause That Spoke Volumes

The room was quiet.

Dr. Amir Patel and his patient, Reed, sat across from each other. Reed had just shared something raw—his fear of being "a burden" to anyone who got too close. Then he went silent.

Amir felt the urge rise: to ask a follow-up question, to soften the silence, to do something.

But this time, he didn't.

He stayed still. Stayed curious. Stayed present.

And then, out of the quiet, Reed whispered, "Most people don't wait."

That was all. But it was everything.

What happened in that moment wasn't just therapeutic. It was transformative. Not because of what was said, but because of what wasn't rushed.

The silence held something sacred.

It held Reed's truth.

And Amir's restraint made it safe.

This is the space between us.

The invisible terrain where healing takes root.

Scene Two: Presence Over Performance

Dr. Elena Martinez used to believe she had to do something to be helpful — interpret, guide, advise. But after her experience with Troy, her resistant patient, something had changed.

She began experimenting with a new question, one she asked herself before every session:

"Can I simply be with this person, without needing to change them?"

With her next patient, a teenage girl named Sasha, she practiced just that.

Sasha talked about nothing and everything — her grades, her mother's boyfriend, her friends who ghosted her, her exhaustion. It was a spiral. A fog.

Elena didn't organize it. She didn't redirect. She didn't analyze.

She just stayed with it.

And near the end of the session, Sasha looked up and said, "This is the first place I talk and don't feel judged."

Elena hadn't done much.

But she had done the hardest thing:

She had stayed present, without performance.

What Lives in the Space Between

Every therapeutic relationship is a shared emotional field — a space shaped by tone, posture, silence, words, memories, and mutual nervous systems.

This is the space where projections play out, where patterns reenact themselves, and where awareness can interrupt what once seemed inevitable.

In this space live questions we may never speak aloud:

- Can I trust you?
- Will you leave me?
- Will you see me and still stay?
- Will you stop needing me to be someone I'm not?

This space holds what Bion called "O"—the unknowable truth we sit with, rather than try to name too quickly.

It holds what Winnicott meant by "holding"—not just in action, but in being.

It is where the patient discovers themselves—not because we gave them answers, but because we made it safe enough for the answers to emerge on their own.

Holding Versus Fixing

To hold space is not to withhold insight. It is to delay intervention until it becomes invited rather than imposed.

It is to ask:

- Am I reacting, or responding?
- Am I intervening because they need it—or because I need to feel effective?

The space between us becomes therapeutic when it is grounded in:

- Clarity instead of control
- Empathy instead of urgency
- Curiosity instead of assumption

The Patient Feels the Difference

Patients may not always know what theories we use, or which modality we've trained in. But they know how we are with them.

They feel it:

- When we are straining to fix them.
- When we are subtly judging them.
- When we are projecting something old onto something new.
- And most importantly — when we are simply with them, clean and clear, honest and human.

It's in the space between us that the real work happens.

Not because of what we do.

But because of who we are willing to be.

In the next chapter, we'll explore how the stories of our past shape how we respond in the present — and how, through the therapeutic relationship, those old stories can begin to be rewritten.

It's where the clinician's healing becomes inseparable from the work itself.

Chapter 11: Lessons from the Past, Healing in the Present

Scene One: The Story Beneath the Response

Dr. Evelyn Carter hadn't planned on crying in supervision.

But as she described a moment with her patient, Miriam—who had recently canceled two sessions in a row and returned, overly apologetic, eager to "be good"—the tears came.

"It's not her," Evelyn said, voice cracking. "It's… how I felt. Like I was the one who had done something wrong."

Her supervisor didn't speak right away. Just nodded slowly.

"Who taught you that being abandoned meant you had failed?"

The question hit hard.

Evelyn didn't answer—not with words, at least. But she saw it:

Her childhood. Her mother's sudden emotional withdrawals. The uncertainty that always followed. The hours spent trying to figure out what she had done wrong, how to fix it, how to be better.

And now, years later, when Miriam disappeared and returned, Evelyn wasn't reacting to her patient.

She was reacting to the echo of her younger self.

Scene Two: The Clinician's Inner Child

Dr. Amir Patel sat in session with a client who struggled with authority—someone who lashed out when asked to take responsibility, who turned every invitation into a perceived attack.

And Amir felt it again: that tightening in his chest, the unspoken You don't get to speak to me that way.

He had always assumed this reaction was about boundaries. But when he slowed down and traced the feeling, he found something else:

A memory of his high school teacher, the one who mocked him in front of the class. The helpless fury he had swallowed. The part of him that had vowed to never be spoken down to again.

And now, when his patient raised his voice or challenged him, Amir didn't just feel threatened—he felt small.

That wasn't the patient's fault.

That was Amir's past, whispering through the present.

Scene Three: Lisa's Breakthrough

Lisa Moreno was walking home from her office when it hit her.

The weight she had been carrying—the guilt of not being able to "reach" her most difficult patients—was not new.

It was the same guilt she had carried at twelve, when her mother relapsed again after rehab. The same helplessness. The same self-blame.

No one had told her it was her job to fix her mother. But no one had told her it wasn't.

And so, unconsciously, she had become the fixer. The rescuer. The over-functioner in every room.

Now, as a therapist, she carried that same silent vow into her work: If I just say the right thing, they'll get better. If they don't, it's because I failed.

But now, for the first time, she saw it clearly.

And that clarity changed everything.

Healing Happens in Both Directions

We think of therapy as something we give to others.

But over time, every clinician who pays attention discovers something else:

The work we do with our patients becomes a mirror for our own unfinished work.

Each emotional response, each familiar ache, each unexpected moment of tenderness or anger—these are not interruptions.

They are invitations to look inward.

To grieve.

To forgive.

To remember.

To grow.

Our patients are not here to heal us.

But in the sacred space of therapy, healing can happen in both directions—if we let it.

The Dual Journey

This is the paradox: the more self-aware we become, the more available we are to others.

- When we stop reacting from the past, we meet the present with new eyes.
- When we name our projections, we interrupt the reenactments.
- When we allow ourselves to be moved, we move the work forward.

Therapy becomes less about control and more about connection.

Less about fixing, more about witnessing.

Less about leading, more about accompanying.

It becomes a dual journey:

One where the clinician's self-awareness becomes the soil in which trust can grow.

And where every therapeutic encounter becomes a living reminder that we, too, are still becoming.

In Part III, we will turn our focus to the science that underpins this emotional landscape—the neuroscience of projection, the role of mirror neurons, and the biological transformation that comes with true presence and self-awareness.

Part III: The Science and Practice of Self-Awareness

Chapter 12: The Neuroscience of Projection

Scene One: What the Brain Sees Isn't What's There

Dr. Lisa Moreno sat with her coffee, reading a research article she had bookmarked weeks ago but never made time to open.

The title read:

"Perception as Prediction: How the Brain Constructs Reality."

It wasn't a catchy headline. But as she read, something clicked.

The article summarized a central finding in modern neuroscience:

We don't perceive the world as it is. We perceive it as the brain expects it to be.

Sensory information comes in, yes—but it's fragmentary, messy.

The brain fills in the blanks based on prior experience.

It doesn't just record reality. It constructs it.

And that's when Lisa realized:

Projection isn't just psychological.

It's biological.

The Predictive Brain

According to leading neuroscientists like Karl Friston and Anil Seth, the brain is a prediction machine.

Rather than waiting for reality to arrive, the brain creates a constant stream of predictions about what is likely to happen—and then adjusts based on incoming data.

These predictions are influenced by memory, emotion, learning, and repetition.

In other words:

What we expect shapes what we perceive.

And often, our expectations are rooted in the past.

This is why one patient's silence might feel soothing to one clinician—and threatening to another.

It's not just the silence.

It's the meaning the brain attaches to it, based on everything it has learned before.

Mirror Neurons: Feeling What We See

Discovered in the early 1990s by researchers in Parma, Italy, mirror neurons are brain cells that activate both when we perform an action and when we observe someone else perform that action.

This discovery changed everything.

- Because it means:
    - When your patient winces, a part of your brain winces, too.
    - When they look away in shame, your body feels the contraction, even if you don't consciously name it.
    - When they light up in joy, your brain lights up, too.

We are wired to resonate with others.

But here's the twist:

The brain doesn't always distinguish between what is happening now and what happened before.

So when a patient's tone resembles a critical parent, or their story echoes your own losses, your brain might respond not to them—but to your history.

That's projection.

And it happens at the level of neurons.

Emotional Memory and Reactivity

The amygdala is the brain's threat detector.

It doesn't think. It doesn't reason. It simply scans for danger.

But it has a bias: it responds not to logic, but to emotional memory.

If a patient raises their voice and it reminds you of a past trauma, your amygdala doesn't wait for confirmation. It sounds the alarm.

Before you even register the thought, your body is responding.

Maybe you feel tense. Defensive. Maybe your heart races.

This is not weakness.

This is wiring.

But if we remain unaware of these responses, we might unconsciously act from them—redirecting the conversation, shutting down the patient, or withdrawing emotionally.

Self-awareness doesn't override the amygdala.

It re-educates it.

Neuroplasticity: Why Self-Awareness Heals

The good news? The brain can change.

Thanks to neuroplasticity, the more we practice awareness—pausing, noticing, reflecting—the more we build new pathways for regulation, insight, and presence.

Clinicians who learn to track their emotional responses in real time begin to rewire not only their reactions, but their relationships.

Each moment of non-reactivity, each breath before responding, each time we say, "What is this really about?" — these are not just psychological acts.

They are neural interventions.

They reshape the circuitry.

They break old loops.

They open new doors.

The Clinician's Brain, Transformed

This is what neuroscience teaches us:

- Projection is not a failure of training. It is a feature of being human.
- Our past shapes our perception at the level of biology.
- But awareness—moment by moment—has the power to change the structure of the brain itself.

And the more we practice, the more our presence becomes a healing signal to others.

Patients feel when we are present.

Not just because of what we say—but because of how we resonate.

We become the safety they didn't know they needed.

Not because we say the right thing.

But because we are not caught in the past.

And that, above all, is the gift of a rewired mirror.

In the next chapter, we'll explore how to use projection deliberately—as a clinical tool. We'll look at how to recognize it, work with it, and when appropriate, even share its insights with patients.

Chapter 13: Using Projection as a Clinical Tool

Scene One: From Trigger to Tool

Dr. Evelyn Carter had once seen projection as something to avoid. A bias. A blind spot. Something she needed to manage quietly and internally.

But after years of doing the deeper work—of tracking her emotional responses, understanding her personal history, and noticing how her past shaped her presence—she began to see it differently.

Projection wasn't a problem to solve.

It was a tool to use.

A message.

A signal.

A flashlight pointing toward something important—either about the patient, or about herself, or about what was unfolding in the space between them.

And if she paid attention—without judgment, without urgency—she could learn to work with it.

Recognizing the Projection in Real Time

Lisa Moreno had developed a simple three-question framework that lived quietly on a sticky note inside her notebook:

1. What am I feeling right now?
2. Is this feeling familiar—from somewhere outside this room?
3. What role am I playing that I didn't consciously agree to?

She didn't use it every session. She didn't always need to.

But when she noticed herself leaning in too quickly, feeling irritated without clear cause, or fantasizing about "saving" someone—she returned to these questions.

Often, they led her to something profound.

Sometimes they reminded her of a wound.

Sometimes they revealed an assumption.

Sometimes they showed her how she was stepping into an old dynamic—one that didn't belong to the present moment.

And once she saw it, she could choose differently.

Techniques for Working with Projection

The following practices emerged from the work of seasoned clinicians who turned self-reflection into a discipline.

Each technique is simple. None are easy. But all are powerful.

1. The Micropause

Before responding to emotionally charged moments, take a breath.

Not a metaphorical breath—a literal one.

This activates the parasympathetic nervous system and gives space for awareness to arise.

Even 2–3 seconds can interrupt automatic projection.

2. Naming the Narrative (Internally First)

When you feel a familiar emotional reaction, silently name it:

"I feel dismissed."

"I feel like a failure."

"I feel unseen."

Then ask: Is this coming from the patient—or from me?

This moment of internal naming creates a boundary between reality and reenactment.

3. Decoding Emotional Intensity

The stronger the emotional response, the more likely a projection is at play.

Disproportionate frustration, admiration, protectiveness, or urgency often point to something deeper.

Use intensity as a cue, not as proof of correctness.

4. Tracking the Role You're In

If you feel like the parent, the savior, the rejected child, the punished partner—pause.

Ask: Who am I becoming in this moment?

That question alone can reorient you to the present.

When (and How) to Share with the Patient

Self-awareness doesn't always need to be shared. But sometimes, when the moment is right, and the relationship is strong, a thoughtful reflection can be transformative.

The key is discernment.

- Noticing a projection is for you.
- Sharing it is for them—only if it deepens the work.

When it feels appropriate, the reflection might sound like:

"Something in me wanted to protect you in that moment, and I'm wondering if that's something people often try to do for you."

Or:

"I noticed I felt unusually frustrated, and I realized it might not be about you. Can we explore what this moment is bringing up for both of us?"

It's not about making it about you.

It's about naming the field that both of you are swimming in.

When done thoughtfully, it models presence, humility, and self-inquiry.

And patients feel that.

They trust it.

Because it tells them: You're not just looking at me. You're looking at yourself, too.

Ethical Considerations

Using projection as a tool must always be grounded in:

- Patient safety
- Therapeutic boundaries
- Commitment to doing your own internal work first

We don't project to patients.

We project onto them, unconsciously.

But we can work with that material consciously—and ethically.

If in doubt, seek consultation or supervision.

If it feels like self-soothing or confessing—don't share it.

If it feels like clarity and service—consider how and when to offer it.

Techniques for Recognizing Personal Projections

Working with projection begins not by confronting it, but by recognizing it. The most effective techniques are those that invite curiosity, not defensiveness. One such tool is the "projection pause"—a moment of mindfulness where we ask, "What if this has more to do with me than with them?" (Segal, 1991). Journaling exercises that trace reactivity, recurring judgments, and emotional triggers can also help bring the unconscious into awareness. In therapeutic settings, techniques from schema therapy, such as imagery rescripting, can surface early unmet needs that drive projections (Young et al., 2003). Free association and dream work, long favored in psychoanalysis, offer indirect yet profound access to the disowned self (Freud, 1900/1953). Whether through mindfulness, journaling, or therapeutic dialogue, the key is to gently peel back the layers—conscious, preconscious, and unconscious—until the projection dissolves into integration.

The Clinical Self as Instrument

Every therapist has been taught that the self is the instrument.

But few are taught how to tune that instrument.

Projection is how the instrument gets warped.

Awareness is how it gets tuned.

When we track ourselves with honesty and compassion, we become clearer, cleaner, more resonant instruments of healing.

And from that place, we no longer fear our emotional responses.

We use them.

In the next chapter, we'll step outside the therapy room—and explore how projection shows up in everyday life, relationships, leadership, and the quiet spaces we don't always recognize as clinical, but which are still filled with mirrors.

Chapter 14: Beyond the Therapy Room

Scene One: The Grocery Line Mirror

Dr. Amir Patel was waiting in line at the store when it happened.

The woman ahead of him was speaking slowly to the cashier, counting change with shaking hands. The line was growing. Someone behind Amir sighed audibly. He felt his jaw clench.

Seriously? This is taking forever.

Then he caught himself.

The thought wasn't unfamiliar.

The irritability wasn't new.

But this time, he paused.

Beneath the frustration was something else—something less comfortable.

Impatience, yes.

But also guilt.

The woman reminded him of his grandmother in her last years—confused, embarrassed by how long everything took. He remembered the shame he felt watching others grow impatient with her.

And now here he was.

Feeling the same impatience.

Not because of the woman.

But because of the unhealed grief he still carried.

Projection Doesn't Clock Out

Therapy may end at the 50-minute mark.

But the mind doesn't.

Projection doesn't wait for a couch, a diagnosis, or a signed consent form.

It happens:

- In meetings
- In friendships
- In families
- At gas stations
- In marriages
- And most often, in silence

We think we're reacting to the moment.

But often, we're reenacting the past.

Scene Two: Elena in the Boardroom

Dr. Elena Martinez was attending a leadership retreat for mental health professionals. One of the facilitators, a woman named Dana, challenged a point Elena made during a discussion.

It was minor. Respectful. Even thoughtful.

But Elena felt herself go cold. Defensive. Dismissed.

She didn't speak again for the rest of the morning.

During lunch, a colleague asked, "Are you okay?"

Elena nodded, but the question stayed with her.

That evening, she reflected.

Why had Dana's comment struck so deep?

And there it was—her older sister's voice. The same critical tone. The same subtle correction. The years of feeling like her ideas were "almost good enough, but not quite."

Dana hadn't silenced her.

Elena had gone silent out of an old reflex.

Relational Triggers Are Everywhere

Projection happens whenever there is emotional charge without clear cause.

When your friend's joke feels like a jab.

When your partner's delay feels like abandonment.

When your child's frustration feels like disrespect.

It's not just the moment.

It's the mirror.

And in these everyday moments, we are given dozens of invitations to pause and ask:

- What story am I reliving?
- What part of me is reacting?
- What would it mean to respond instead of reenact?

Leadership, Supervision, and Projection

In leadership roles, projection can be even more complex.

A supervisee who avoids meetings may unconsciously echo a clinician's memory of being ignored.

A colleague who seeks frequent reassurance might trigger the leader's old fatigue of emotional caretaking.

A team member who challenges authority might awaken buried shame around powerlessness.

And unless we are aware, we might confuse personal discomfort for organizational dysfunction.

Or worse: we might recreate the very systems of harm we hoped to dismantle.

Leaders who become aware of their projections lead differently.

They don't just act.

They reflect.

They learn to distinguish between what's happening in front of them and what's echoing behind them.

And they model what it means to live and work with conscious accountability.

Making the World a Reflective Space

When clinicians begin to use projection awareness beyond the therapy room, a quiet transformation unfolds:

- Conflict becomes feedback.
- Discomfort becomes a doorway.
- Relationships become places of remembering and repair.

We stop needing others to behave so we don't get triggered.

We start using our triggers to become more whole.

This is how the work expands.

Not only in depth, but in reach.

We become clinicians not just in session, but in life.

Not because we interpret everything, but because we meet everything with awareness.

In our final chapter, we'll return to the deepest questions:

What does it mean to live with the mirror always near?

To walk through life seeing every reaction as a teacher?

And to choose, again and again, to reflect rather than project?

Chapter 15: Walking with the Mirror

Scene One: Evelyn's Walk

It was dusk. The sidewalks were quiet.

Dr. Evelyn Carter walked home from her last session of the day, scarf wrapped loosely around her shoulders, the chill of autumn just beginning to settle into the trees.

She passed a couple arguing at the corner.

She heard someone laugh too loudly behind her.

She saw a teenager sitting on the curb, head buried in their arms.

And she noticed herself noticing.

Noticing what each moment stirred in her—what arose in her body before her mind made meaning of it.

The mirror was everywhere.

And for once, she wasn't overwhelmed by it.

She was walking with it.

Seeing as a Daily Practice

To live with the mirror is not to be in constant analysis.

It is to walk with curiosity.

To notice:

- The tightness in your chest during a conversation.
- The urge to defend your worth in a meeting.
- The softness that rises in you when someone dares to be real.

It is to ask gently, What is this showing me about me?

And then to listen—not for blame, but for insight.

Self-awareness is not perfection.

It is presence.

And presence, once cultivated, radiates.

It heals in quiet, consistent ways.

From Reaction to Responsibility

Responsibility doesn't mean fault.

It means the ability to respond—rather than react.

When we see our projections clearly, we begin to reclaim agency.

We stop needing others to act differently in order to feel okay.

We start noticing what needs attention within.

And from that place, we become more honest, more available, more whole.

This is the deep work.

The lifelong work.

Not just for the patient.

For the clinician.

For the human.

Every Patient a Mirror

Every patient becomes a reflection—not just of suffering, but of our opportunity to grow.

- The one who challenges your competence.
- The one who activates your grief.
- The one who mirrors your childhood home.
- The one who reminds you of who you used to be—or who you're afraid to become.

Each one, a mirror.

Each one, an invitation.

And every time you meet it with honesty, something in you shifts.

And so does something in them.

This is the ripple.

This is the mirror's quiet magic.

Closing Reflections

Walking with the Mirror

To be a clinician is to witness the suffering of others—and, often unknowingly, the echoes of our own.

Throughout this book, we've explored what it means to treat projection not as pathology, but as a portal. We've seen how emotional reactions, unconscious patterns, and even therapeutic "missteps" can become tools of profound insight—when we are willing to look inward with honesty, humility, and care.

From Freud's early observations of transference and countertransference to Jung's assertion that what irritates us in others is a clue to our own unfinished business, we've revisited these foundational truths not as static theories, but as living realities. The science of today—mirror neurons, emotional contagion, and the predictive brain—only confirms what the great thinkers intuited: the world is not happening to us; it is happening through us.

This is not just theory. It is practice. In every moment of tension with a patient, in every feeling that catches you off guard, in every impulse to withdraw, to fix, to prove—you are being offered a mirror. A chance to pause. A chance to ask: What is this moment asking of me? What part of me is being touched?

This is not easy work. But it is sacred work. And it is lifelong. Because the clinician who is willing to reflect becomes more than a helper—they become a presence. And presence is what heals.

So as you return to your sessions, your consultations, your supervision, and your inner life, we invite you to keep the mirror close. Not to judge yourself—but to know yourself. To grow, not in spite of your reactivity, but because of it.

Let your projections become your teachers. Let your reactions guide your inquiry. Let your discomfort awaken your deepest compassion. And above all, may you never forget:

The mirror is never the patient.

The mirror is never the work.

The mirror is always, and only, you.

And that is where the healing begins.

Every reaction is a message. Every moment is a mirror. And every mirror is an invitation—to return to yourself.

Epilogue: You Were Always in the Room

The mirror was never just a metaphor.

It was always there, quietly reflecting back the parts of us we didn't yet know how to see.

Every sigh we misunderstood. Every silence that unsettled us. Every frustration, every moment of impatience, every unspoken sense of defeat. Each one was an invitation.

Not a flaw in the work; but a portal into it.

Throughout this book, we have followed clinicians not as experts, but as human beings—vulnerable, complex, and in process. Their journeys are not separate from yours. They are yours. They are ours. Because to be a clinician is not to heal from outside the story, but to learn from within it.

In the end, it was never about fixing. It was never about perfect neutrality. It was about presence; and about the courage to stay, when the mirror reveals more than we expected.

This work asks of us something sacred:

To notice our reactions.

To hold them with care.

To meet ourselves with the same compassion we offer others.

And when we forget—because we will forget—

the mirror waits. It does not judge. It does not accuse. It simply reflects. And with each glance, each recognition, each moment of quiet awareness, we remember:

That healing was never meant to be one-sided.

That growth does not end with licensure.

And that self-awareness is not a luxury in our field— it is the practice.

So, if you ever find yourself wondering what's happening in the room, ask not only what the patient is showing you; but what you are showing yourself.

And in that reflection, may you always find a guide.

And a home.

You were always in the room.

Now, you know why.

Final Reflection

Standing with the Mirror

Before you close this book, take a breath.

Let the room become quiet.

Let your mind settle—not into what comes next, but into what's already here.

Now, ask yourself:

- What patient, past or present, has stirred something in you that you didn't yet understand?
- What feelings still linger after sessions—frustration, urgency, irritation, tenderness, fear?
- What are those feelings trying to teach you about you?

And now, go deeper:

- When have you mistaken your own history for the present moment?
- Where are your patterns reappearing, asking not to be judged—but to be held?
- What do you avoid feeling in your work—and what does that avoidance protect?

Pause again.

Not to fix. Not to change.

But to notice. And name.

"Every reaction is a mirror. Every mirror is an invitation."

As you continue your work—session by session, hour by hour—may you return often to this quiet place.

To the inner room behind the outer room.

To the sacred space where clinician becomes witness, and presence becomes transformation.

You are not separate from the work.

You are the work.

And the work begins—with you.

A Final Invitation to You, the Reader

Dear Reader,

Thank you for walking with us through these pages—not just as a clinician, but as a human being willing to look inward.

This book was not meant to offer all the answers. It was meant to hold up a mirror—to reveal what's often overlooked, to illuminate the spaces within us that still seek understanding, and to remind us that our most powerful tool in this work is not our knowledge, but our presence.

We invite you now to pause and reflect:

- What has shifted in you?
- What do you now see differently—in your work, in your relationships, in yourself?
- What reaction surprised you most, and what might it be pointing toward?
- What mirror will you carry forward into your next session?

If this journey has touched you, challenged you, or helped you grow, we ask one small thing:

Share it.

Tell a colleague. Recommend it to your supervision group. Use it as a springboard for deeper conversations. Healing expands when it is named.

And if it feels right, we'd be honored if you would leave a brief review wherever you found this book. Your reflection may be the mirror someone else needs to begin their own journey.

This work is never finished. But with each moment of awareness, with each breath of presence, we get closer to becoming clinicians—and people—who truly see.

With deep gratitude,

The Authors

Final Acknowledgments

As we close this journey, we are reminded that healing—whether personal or professional—is not a destination, but a path we walk again and again, with increasing honesty and grace.

We want to thank the editorial team, peer reviewers, and early readers whose insights sharpened our clarity and deepened our conviction that this work matters.

To our loved ones, who supported us through late nights, hard truths, and vulnerable storytelling—your presence behind the scenes made every word possible. Thank you for holding us when we needed to be held.

To the many clinicians across disciplines who engage in this work with courage: may you continue to use your reactions not as signs of failure, but as invitations to wholeness.

And finally, to the mirror itself—ever present, ever patient—we thank you for reminding us that the greatest work we do in the world always begins within.

Reader Integration Toolkit

The Clinician's Mirror: A Story of Projection, Self-Discovery, and Healing

A Practical Bridge from Message to Implementation

1. Daily Reflection Prompts: One-Minute Mirror Practice

Use at the end of a session or your clinical day:

- What moment stirred something in me today?
- What did I feel most strongly—and what does that say about me?
- What did I avoid or dismiss? Why?
- Was there a moment I judged my patient or myself? What belief lies beneath that judgment?
- What part of my personal history may have been present in the room?

2. Weekly Clinician Mirror Journal

Choose one question per week to explore deeply:

- What patient reaction do I find most difficult, and why?
- What themes do I notice across the patients who trigger me?
- Where in my personal life does this pattern appear?
- What might this reaction be trying to protect?
- How can I use this awareness to deepen the therapeutic alliance?

3. Supervision and Peer Consultation Questions

Bring these to clinical supervision, group case review, or peer reflection:

- What part of this patient's behavior resonates with my own internal experience?

- What feelings do I leave with after sessions—and what might they indicate?
- When I feel "stuck," what part of myself might also be stuck?
- What do I wish the patient would do—and what does that wish reveal about my needs or fears?

4. Mirror Awareness Framework (M.A.F.)

1. A 3-step model to identify and work with projection:
   (1) Notice
2. Pause. What are you feeling right now? Label it. Own it.
3. (2) Inquire
4. Ask: "What part of me is being touched or activated in this moment?"
5. (3) Integrate
6. Reflect: "How can I hold space for this part of me while still being fully present for the patient?"

5. Self-Compassion Practice

1. Use when self-judgment, shame, or reactivity arise:
2. "This is a moment of awareness.
3. I choose to respond with curiosity, not criticism.
4. What I feel does not make me less of a clinician—it makes me more human."

6. Implementation Goals

1. Set one intention each week:
2. This week, I will pause before reacting.
3. This week, I will journal about one difficult session.
4. This week, I will reflect on one pattern that keeps showing up.
5. This week, I will name one part of myself I often avoid in session.

7. Share Your Journey

1. Reflection is more powerful in community.
2. Share insights with colleagues using this toolkit in supervision.
3. Use excerpts or questions during staff retreats, rounds, or peer-led trainings.
4. Start a Mirror Circle—a peer space for self-awareness and support.

8. Keep the Mirror Close

1. This book was just the beginning.
2. The real journey begins now, inside your work, your mind, your relationships—and your heart.

Appendices

Appendix A: Reader Reflection & Discussion Guide

Reflections: The Clinician's Mirror — A Story of Projection, Self-Discovery, and Healing

"Awareness is the first act of freedom."

This guide is meant to be used gently. There are no right answers, only honest ones. Read slowly. Reflect deeply. Journal freely. Discuss with openness; and above all—use your responses as more mirrors.

Projection is not a flaw.

It is a function of how we are built—neurobiologically, psychologically, relationally.

But left unseen, it distorts.

Seen clearly, it transforms.

To walk with the mirror is to walk with reverence.

For the complexity of others.

For the mystery of ourselves.

And for the sacred space in between.

It is to whisper in every interaction:

This feeling is data.

This moment is a teacher.

This work is also my own.

Thank you for walking with us through these stories, reflections, and discoveries.

May this book serve not only as a mirror—but as a companion.

One that reminds you:

The more you see yourself clearly, the more clearly you can see others.

And the more we see each other clearly, the more healing becomes possible.

Part I: The World as a Mirror

1. What reactions—emotional, somatic, or cognitive—did you have while reading the stories of Evelyn, Amir, Lisa, or Elena?

- Did any moment feel uncomfortably familiar?
- Was there a character you felt impatient with? Strongly drawn to? Why?

2. Recall a recent moment in clinical work that stirred something strong in you.

- What do you think was being projected—by your client, and by you?
- Who might that client have unconsciously represented in your internal world?

3. When you think of "the mirror" in your own therapy room, what do you most often see reflected back at you?

- What would happen if you welcomed that reflection rather than resisted it?

Part II: Seeing Ourselves in the Other

4. Think of a time when your self-awareness improved your clinical presence.

- What changed in the room after that insight?
- How did your patient respond?

5. Are there patterns you tend to replay in therapeutic relationships (e.g., rescuing, over-functioning, withdrawing, proving worth)?

- Where do you think that pattern began?
- What would interrupting that pattern feel like—for you and your client?

6. What ripples have you noticed outside of therapy since be-coming more aware of projection?

- In your friendships?
- In your leadership or family roles?

Part III: The Science and Practice of Self-Awareness

7. What did you learn about your own nervous system or brain through the neuroscience of projection?

- How might you begin working with your biology ra-ther than against it in moments of reactivity?

8. Which tools or practices from Chapter 13 most resonated with you?

- Do you already use any of them?
- Which ones might you begin to integrate more intention-ally?

9. Where in your life are you still projecting without knowing it?

- What might it take to become more curious, and less defensive, about what you see in others?

Closing Reflection: Walking with the Mirror

- In what ways has this book changed how you see your patients?
- In what ways has it changed how you see yourself?
- What would it mean for you to live and practice as some-one who walks with the mirror, every day?

"The world will ask you who you are.

And if you do not know,

you will answer with what you are not."

—Carl Jung (paraphrased)

Appendix B: Facilitator's Guide

For Reflective Practice Groups, Supervision Teams, and Learning Cohorts

Based on The Clinician's Mirror — A Story of Projection, Self-Discovery, and Healing

"Facilitating reflection is not about having answers. It's about making space for deeper questions."

Purpose of This Guide

This guide is designed to support group leaders—clinical supervisors, educators, training directors, or peer facilitators—in creating brave, generative spaces where clinicians can reflect deeply on the themes of projection, self-awareness, presence, and healing.

The goal is not to master content, but to practice inner seeing—together.

Structure Overview

You may use this book as:

- A 3-part monthly series (1 part per month)
- A 6-week or 8-week series (1–2 chapters per session)
- A retreat-style intensive (half-day or full-day)
- Ongoing integration across clinical supervision

Each session includes:

1. Opening Moment (2–5 minutes)
2. Selected Reading or Summary
3. Guided Reflection
4. Shared Dialogue
5. Personal Integration Practice

Facilitation Principles

- **Safety First:** Begin every session by grounding the group in confidentiality, compassion, and non-judgment.

- **Model Vulnerability:** Share your own experiences honestly (and humbly) to set the tone.

- **Invite, Don't Extract:** Never pressure participation—create an atmosphere where insight is allowed, not required.

- **Track Process, Not Just Content:** Stay curious about emotional undercurrents in the group. Are certain stories evoking defensiveness? Silence? Laughter? Those are mirrors, too.

- **Pace with the Nervous System:** Slow down when the conversation gets tender or charged. Silence is generative.

Suggested Session Format (60–90 minutes)

1. Opening Moment (2–5 minutes)

Begin with a centering practice, such as:

- One minute of silence
- A breath awareness moment
- A short poem (e.g., Rilke, Rumi, Naomi Shihab Nye)
- A quote from Jung, Freud, or the book itself

Example:

"The mirror holds no lies."

What is one feeling you're noticing right now that you might normally hide?

2. Shared Reading or Recap (5–10 minutes)

Option A: Read a 1–2 paragraph excerpt aloud.

Option B: Briefly summarize a scene or chapter.

Option C: Invite a group member to choose a passage that moved them.

3. Guided Reflection (10–15 minutes)

Choose 2–3 questions from the Reader Reflection Guide, or ask:

- What stirred something in you?
- Where do you recognize yourself in the story?
- Was there a projection you've experienced like this one?

Encourage journaling for a few minutes before discussion.

4. Dialogue and Sharing (30–45 minutes)

Open the floor for stories, insights, questions. Use gentle prompts:

- "Say more about that."
- "Is that a familiar feeling?"
- "Who else has experienced something similar?"

If strong emotions arise, welcome them without analysis. The group is not for interpretation. It is for integration.

5. Integration Practice (5–10 minutes)

End with a closing reflection. Suggestions:

- One word you're taking with you
- One intention for the week ahead
- A short centering breath and release
- Journaling prompt: What am I now more curious about within myself?

Facilitator's Tips by Chapter Theme

- Part I: Focus on emotional recognition, body-based awareness, and the origin of early projections. Normalize discomfort.

- Part II: Emphasize the ripple—how insight deepens not just therapy, but presence in the world. Begin to ask: Where else does this show up in my life?

- Part III: Ground the group in compassion. Talk about neurobiology without jargon. Celebrate the commitment to reflection as a form of clinical rigor and relational integrity.

Optional Group Rituals

- The Mirror Bowl: Place a small bowl in the center of the table. Each session, invite participants to write one insight or question on a small paper and place it inside. Read a few aloud to close.

- "This Week's Mirror": Begin each session with one participant sharing a personal or clinical moment where they noticed projection or self-awareness in action.

Closing the Series

Conclude the final session with gratitude. You might invite:

- One-way participants have changed
- One mirror they now see more clearly
- One story they will carry forward

And always: ONE THING

"What will you now do differently, simply because you saw more clearly?"

Recommended Reading

On Projection, Countertransference, and the Therapeutic Relationship

- Carl Jung – Aion: Researches into the Phenomenology of the Self
- Sigmund Freud – The Neuro-Psychoses of Defence
- Nancy McWilliams – Psychoanalytic Diagnosis: Understanding Personality Structure in the Clinical Process
- Patrick Casement – On Learning from the Patient
- Thomas Ogden – Subjects of Analysis
- James Masterson – The Search for the Real Self
- Karen Maroda – The Power of Countertransference: Innovations in Analytic Technique

Neuroscience, Perception, and Emotional Processing

- Lisa Feldman Barrett – How Emotions Are Made: The Secret Life of the Brain
- Antonio Damasio – The Feeling of What Happens: Body and Emotion in the Making of Consciousness
- V.S. Ramachandran – The Tell-Tale Brain
- Daniel J. Siegel – The Developing Mind
- Stephen Porges – The Polyvagal Theory

Mindfulness, Presence, and Reflective Practice

- Jon Kabat-Zinn – Wherever You Go, There You Are
- Jack Kornfield – A Path with Heart
- Tara Brach – Radical Acceptance
- Mark Epstein, MD – The Trauma of Everyday Life
- Christopher Germer – The Mindful Path to Self-Compassion

Therapist as Person and Healer

- Irvin D. Yalom – The Gift of Therapy
- Louis Cozolino – The Making of a Therapist
- Jeffrey A. Kottler – On Being a Therapist
- Ghislaine Boulanger – Wounded by Reality: Understanding and Treating Adult Onset Trauma
- Philip Bromberg – Standing in the Spaces: Essays on Clinical Process, Trauma, and Dissociation

Therapeutic Growth and the Human Condition

- Viktor E. Frankl – Man's Search for Meaning
- Carl Rogers – On Becoming a Person
- Bessel van der Kolk – The Body Keeps the Score
- Brené Brown – The Gifts of Imperfection
- bell hooks – All About Love: New Visions

Suggested Articles & Essays

- "Countertransference and the Self" by Glen Gabbard (Journal of the American Psychoanalytic Association)
- "The Use of the Self in Psychotherapy" by Harry Stack Sullivan
- "The Unthought Known" by Christopher Bollas

More from SWEET Institute Publishing

Transformational Books for a Transformational World

At SWEET Institute Publishing, we believe in the power of inner transformation to ignite systemic change. Our books are written by clinicians, educators, healers, and thought leaders committed to bridging science and soul, insight and action, healing and justice.

Explore more titles in our growing library:

Before Anything Else, Validate (Coming Soon)

A powerful manifesto and practical guide to using validation as the foundation for healing, relationships, and change—in therapy, leadership, and everyday life.

The Courage to Care

A heart-opening anthology of stories from over 50 social workers reflecting on healing, hope, and the power of human connection in clinical practice.

The Power of Belief

How belief shapes behavior, identity, and outcomes—and how clinicians can help rewrite the beliefs that limit healing and growth.

Rewriting the Script (Coming Soon)

A journey into the internalized narratives we carry—and how to transform shame, internalized oppression, and conditioned roles through therapeutic storytelling.

Time to Heal (Coming Soon)

A revolutionary time management and leadership guide for clinicians, blending neuroscience, psychotherapy, and the art of sustainable change.

How Life Works (Coming Soon)

An inspiring guide to uncovering the lessons in every experience—blending science, spirituality, and storytelling to help readers turn challenges into catalysts.

The Anchor Blueprint (Coming Soon)

A groundbreaking model for caring for high-acuity populations—moving beyond crisis and compliance to healing-centered, layered care.

Stay Connected

Visit us at: SweetInstitutePublishing.com

Sign up for updates, author events, and exclusive early releases.

Follow us on LinkedIn and Facebook

Have a book inside you?

We help clinicians, healers, and educators become published authors.

Email us at: contact@sweetinstitute.com

About the Authors

Mardoche Sidor, MD

Dr. Sidor is a Harvard- and Columbia-trained psychiatrist, quadruple board-certified in General Psychiatry, Child and Adolescent Psychiatry, Forensic Psychiatry, and Addiction Psychiatry. He also holds additional training in Public and Community Psychiatry and Geriatric Psychiatry. Formerly an Assistant Clinical Professor of Psychiatry at Columbia University, he is currently affiliated with the Columbia University Center for Psychoanalytic Study and Research. As the founder of the SWEET Institute, he has dedicated his career to transforming mental health care through education, empowerment, and systemic change. His work integrates psychoanalytic insight, scientific rigor, and a lifelong commitment to human dignity.

Lorie Meiselman, LCSW-R

Lorie Meiselman is a senior clinician, teacher, and integrative therapist with over 30 years of experience across clinical modalities. As senior member at the SWEET Institute, she is known for her deeply embodied presence, authenticity, and wide-ranging expertise—from psychodynamic psychotherapy and cognitive-behavioral therapy to dance/movement therapy and logotherapy. Laurie brings a uniquely holistic perspective to clinical work, blending depth, creativity, and consciousness-based approaches. Her private practice integrates the art and science of healing, and she continues to mentor and inspire clinicians across the country.

Karen Dubin, PhD, LCSW

Dr. Dubin is a clinical social worker, educator, and writer whose work centers on healing, meaning-making, and reflective practice. With a PhD in Social Work and decades of experience as a clinician and supervisor, she is known for blending narrative depth with grounded clinical strategy. As the co-founder of the SWEET Institute, she leads innovative training and publishing initiatives that support clinicians in moving from knowledge to transformation. Dr. Dubin's writing is characterized by its warmth, clarity, and commitment to the inner life of the healer.